Macdonald of Kingston

Macdonald of Kingston.
First Prime Minister

by Donald Swainson

A Personal Library
Publication, produced
exclusively for

Nelson

Macdonald of Kingston

Personal Library,
Publishers
Suite 539,
17 Queen Street East
Toronto, Canada M5C 1P9

A Personal Library publication
produced exclusively for
Thomas Nelson & Sons (Canada) Limited
81 Curlew Drive, Don Mills, Ontario
M3A 2R1

Publisher: Glenn Edward Witmer
Editor: Claire Gerus
Designer: Jonathan Milne
Researcher: C. Van Baren

Canadian Cataloguing in Publication Data

Swainson, Donald, 1938–
Macdonald of Kingston

(Canada's Heritage in Pictures)

Bibliography: p.6
Includes index.
ISBN 0-17-600739-3

1. Macdonald, John Alexander, Sir, 1815-1891.
2. Prime ministers–Canada–Biography.
3 Canada–Politics and government–19th century.
I. Title. II. Series.

FC521.M3S93   971.05'4'0924   C79-094042-6
F1033.M13S93

To The Memory Of Lieutenant-Colonel
Arthur Kristjan Swainson, 1931-1978.

Other books by the author:

Ontario and Confederation–Ontario et la Confédération (Centennial Commission: Historical Booklet No. 5)

The Prime Ministers of Canada (with Christopher Ondaatje), (Pagurian Press)

Historical Essays on the Prairie Provinces (Editor), (McClelland & Stewart Limited)

John A. Macdonald: The Man and the Politician, (Oxford University Press)

The Last Forty Years: The Union of 1841 to Confederation by J. C. Dent (Editor), (McClelland & Stewart Limited)

Oliver Mowat's Ontario (Editor), (Macmillan Company of Canada Ltd.)

Acknowledgments
Much generous assistance was received while this book was being prepared. The staffs of several archives were helpful and pleasant while the search for illustrations was pursued. I would like to thank those people who assisted at the Public Archives of Canada, Queen's University Archives, Bellevue House, Kingston (Parks Canada), Public Archives of Ontario and Public Archives of Manitoba. I would also like to thank William Teatero for assisting in the search for photographs. John Brebner took some new photographs in Kingston, and photographed several artifacts in the Queen's University Archives. Mrs. May Forrester, Department of History, Queen's University, assisted in a variety of ways.

Numerous quotations from original sources are scattered throughout the book. They are excerpted from the usual places: archival materials, newspapers, memoirs, collections of documents, published letters, parliamentary debates and electioneering materials. A number of these quotations, some of which are famous, appear elsewhere and have been cited from published material. I am, of course, profoundly indebted to the numerous and excellent scholars who have studied Canada during the Macdonald era. The quotation that ends the volume is from a Macdonald speech six years before Confederation when he was discussing the Province of Canada. This 1861 statement has about it a timeless quality. It characterized Macdonald's attitude towards the Dominion of Canada, and would no doubt represent his sentiments if he were with us today.

Further Reading

There is a vast quantity of literature that relates to Sir John A. Macdonald and his Canada. The most important work is D.G. Creighton's vast biography, *John A. Macdonald, 2 vols. (Toronto, 1952 and 1955). A much shorter study is Donald Swainson, *John A. Macdonald: The Man and the Politician (Toronto, 1971). E.B. Biggar, Anecdotal Life of Sir John Macdonald (Montreal, 1891) contains hundreds of fascinating stories. Several volumes of Macdonald's letters have been published. Joseph Pope, Correspondence of Sir John Alexander Macdonald (Toronto, 1921) is concerned for the most part with his public life. J.K. Johnson, *Affectiona-tely Yours: The Letters of Sir John A. Macdonald and his Family (Toronto, 1969) is concerned with the private lives of Macdonald and his close relatives.

It is not possible to understand Macdonald without a knowledge of Kingston. Three books provide a good introduction to Macdonald's town: James A. Roy, Kingston: The King's Town (Toronto, 1952); Margaret Angus, The Old Stones of Kingston: Its Buildings Before 1867 (Toronto, 1966) and, Gerald Tulchinsky, ed., To Preserve and Defend: Essays on Kingston in the Nineteenth Century (Montreal, 1976).

Macdonald's colleagues and opponents are important. There are scores of books and articles on these men. The best is easily J.M.S. Care-less, *Brown of the Globe, 2 vols. (Toronto, 1959, 1963).

Many other of Sir John's contemporaries can be studied in numerous excellent articles in the appropriate volumes of the Dictionary of Cana-dian Biography. Amongst many other studies in the D.C.B. are articles on G.E. Cartier, T.D. McGee, John Sand-field Macdonald, J.H. Cameron, Joseph Howe and Lord Elgin.

Confederation has been much studied. For Macdonald's role see P.B. Waite, *The Life and Times of Confederation, 1864-1867 (Toronto, 1962); D.G. Creighton, *The Road to Confederation (Toronto, 1964); Donald Swainson, *Ontario and Confederation (Ottawa, 1967).

For general back-ground see Kenneth McNaught, *The Pelican History of Canada (Markham, 1976) The appropriate volumes in The Canadian Cente-nary Series provide a comprehensive survey of Canada, 1841-96. They are J.M.S. Careless, *The Union of the Canadas, 1841-1857 (Toronto, 1967); W.L. Morton, *The Critical Years, 1857-1873 (Toronto, 1964); and, P.B. Waite, *Canada 1874-1896: Arduous Destiny (Toronto, 1971).

For the central Canadian background see Mason Wade, *The French Canadians, 1760-1867, 2 vols. (Revised Edition, Toronto, 1968); Donald Swainson, ed., *Oliver Mowat's Ontario (Toronto, 1972); and, Joseph Schull, Ontario Since 1867 (Toronto, 1978).

Books of course cannot tell us everything about Sir John A. Macdonald and his country. One should also view what we have left of his Canada. A particularly fine example is Bellevue House, Kingston.

*paperback books

Preface

This is an entrancing book. To all who read it, it will be a revelation of much that is generally unknown of the life of the First Prime Minister of Canada. It is also evidence that history is better understood for most people when it is in pictures rather than in words.

The book fully establishes that it was Sir John A. Macdonald who was the Father of our Country without whose dedication and determination against great odds, Confederation would not have taken place.

My two political heroes throughout life have been Sir John A. Macdonald and Sir Wilfrid Laurier, both of whom, in the passing years, have become immortalized.

Laurier was Macdonald's political opponent throughout the years and was Leader of the Opposition during Macdonald's last tenure of office. I am one who has developed a deep admiration for those who sit opposite me in the House of Commons and who disagree with me, however strongly. Such was the relationship between Macdonald and Laurier.

Laurier's tribute to Macdonald in the House of Commons the day following the Prime Minister's death is a masterpiece of diction and eloquence.

I shall quote a number of his views:

"His loss overwhelms us. For my part, I say with all truth, his loss overwhelms me, and it also overwhelms this Parliament, as if indeed one of the institutions of the land had given way. Sir John Macdonald now belongs to the ages, and it can be said with certainty, that the career which has just been closed is one of the most remarkable careers of this century."

"Sir John Macdonald was gifted as few men in any land or in any age were gifted; gifted with the most high of all qualities, qualities which would have made him famous wherever exercised and which would have shone all the more conspicuously the larger the theatre."

"He was also endowed with those inner, subtle, undefinable graces of soul which win and keep the hearts of men. As to his statesmanship, it is written in the history of Canada, for he was connected and associated with all the events, all the facts which brought Canada from the position Canada then occupied–the position of two small provinces, having nothing in common but a common allegiance, united by a bond of paper, and united by nothing else–to the present state of development which Canada has reached."

When the publisher of this book asked me to write this Preface, he did not know that Macdonald's parents and my maternal great grandparents, Mr. and Mrs. George Bannerman (Campbell), lived a few miles distant from each other in the Highlands of Caithness. In the early 1800's Macdonald's parents moved to Glasgow where John A. was born, having realized that the Countess of Sutherland who, to use her own words, "preferred sheep to men," sooner or later as she threatened would remove the residents of Kildonan and adjoining areas in order to provide more fodder for sheep. Some years later the Macdonald family migrated to Upper Canada.

My maternal great grandparents, along with 1500 others in Kildonan, were driven from their humble crofts during the barbaric Clearances. In 1813 they joined the Selkirk Settlers and settled temporarily at Fort Churchill. They were driven out in the winter and made their way on foot to York Factory, and then later on with others of the settlers journeyed to their destination on the Red River. In the winter of 1815, they decided that they would take up residence in Upper Canada and made their way on foot to Fort William where scows were constructed to convey them to Upper Canada the following spring.

There are many coincidences in history which almost seem fore-ordained: if it had not been for the Countess of Sutherland and her minions deciding to get rid of the people living in Kildonan and adjoining areas, neither the First nor Thirteenth Prime Ministers of Canada would have been.

Macdonald was the first Canadian to be appointed to her Majesty's Privy Council, thereby entitling him to the designation of 'Right Honourable.' I am now the only living Canadian member of Her Privy Council–and the last because of a decision by the Pearson administration that no further appointments were to be made. Henceforth Privy Council membership would be restricted to the Canadian Privy Council.

Macdonald had his shortcomings of which he was fully and sometimes boastfully aware. As to his alleged over-fondness of whiskey he had a sense of humour, and when criticism (often exaggerated by political opponents) was made in this regard, he turned it to his advantage. A member of a delegation from Montreal who met with him in his office told me of a pertinent incident. The Chairman of the Delegation was the President of the Quebec Temperance Organization, and the other members of the delegation were fearful that he would raise the issue and render it difficult, if not impossible, to attain their objective. As things turned out their fears were unfounded. Macdonald, having seated the delegation with the President to his right, startled all present when he spoke harshly to the President: "Will you get over. You're too close to me. Your breath is positively abominable. It smells of water!" Everybody joined in the laughter and the members of the delegation got what they asked for.

During one of his last campaign meetings Macdonald spoke of being near the end of life and liable to pass away at any time. One of his audience in a loud voice explained: "Sir John, you will never die!" No prophecy ever made has been proven in the light of history to be more accurate. He lives today in the hearts of his countrymen.

As was said of Sir Christopher Wren, when someone asked: "Where is the monument to that great man?"; the reply was: "If you would see his monument, look about you."

Macdonald's monument is Canada!

Rt. Hon. John G. Diefenbaker   December 6, 1978
P.C., C.H., Q.C., M.A., LL.D., D.C.L., M.P.   Ottawa

Foreword

Harvey M. Haber is a Toronto lawyer and fervent advocate of the view that a much greater emphasis should be placed on the study of Canada's past by our schools. He has pursued this goal for many years, and was one of the people who early on encouraged the publisher to proceed with a series of books which will promote that ideal.

I am delighted that this book has been written. It is a tribute to Canada's greatest statesman, the Chief Architect of Confederation and Canada's first Prime Minister.

Sir John A. Macdonald had a vision – a vision which saw, in his own lifetime, the realization of Confederation, the purchase of the western territories from the Hudson's Bay Company, the founding of the Provinces of Manitoba and British Columbia, and the construction of the CPR, which finally linked Canada from sea to sea.

His warmth, affection, tenacity, and respect for his fellow man made these insurmountable goals a reality during a challenging and rocky political career – something only he could achieve.

Through these difficult times, his humour and wit never failed him. He was a formidable debater and enjoyed the banter of the House of Commons sessions. The following encounter between Sir John A. and a fellow parliamentarian is one of my favourites:
"Fellow member:
'The right honourable gentleman has made a statement in a menacing manner, pointing his finger at me, and I call upon him to explain the meaning of it.'
Sir John A.:
'All I can say is, Mr. Speaker, if I pointed my finger at the honourable gentleman, I take my finger back.'"

But he was also, in spite of a lifetime of personal tragedies, a warm and understanding person, as the following anecdote shows.
A little girl, unknown to Sir John, wrote to congratulate him on his seventy-sixth birthday. She mentioned that she had once written to a boy who had not answered her. Therefore, said she, "If you get this letter, do not forget to write if you git it." From Earnscliffe, Sir John's official residence in Ottawa, came the reply:
"My dear little Friend,

I am glad to get your letter, and to know that next Sunday you and I will be of the same age. I hope and believe however that you will see many more birthdays than I shall, and I trust that every birthday may find you strong in health and prosperous and happy.

I think it was mean of that young fellow not to answer your letter. You see, I have been longer in the world than he, and know more than he does of what is due to young ladies.

I send you a dollar note, with which pray buy some small keepsake to remember me by, and believe me,
Yours sincerely
John A. Macdonald"

For some time now I have set for myself the goal of helping to establish a day of tribute for our first prime minister, Sir John A. Macdonald. I encourage consideration of the anniversary of his birth, January 11, for such an annual celebration, a time for recognition, by schools, industry, the media and, indeed, all Canadians who want to honour this great man, the father of our country.

Harvey M. Haber

November 30, 1978
Toronto

9

Introduction

John Alexander Macdonald is a crucial figure in Canadian history, and for well over a hundred years has remained one of our most popular men. It is not difficult to explain why this man has always fascinated Canadians.

Macdonald was a Kingston man, but has been perceived as much more than a local or provincial figure. There are good reasons for this. He was a friend of French Canada and, while George Etienne Cartier was alive, functioned within the most important bi-cultural political partnership in Canadian history. John A. was very much an Ontarian, but nonetheless he fought bitterly with Ontario's leading and representative men. Macdonald's feuds with George Brown, Alexander Mackenzie, Oliver Mowat, and Edward Blake are legendary; at the same time they demonstrated the fact that he was never simply a spokesman for his own province. He represented national interests, even if they collided with those of Ontario. Not surprisingly, many Canadians see Macdonald as a truly national figure. This has added to his popularity in all regions of Canada.

The issues that dominated Macdonald's public life also help explain the perennial interest in his career. Sir John led our first major bi-cultural political party, and struggled to come to terms with the French fact in Canada. It was John A. Macdonald who said of French Canadians, as early as 1856, "Treat them as a nation and they will act as a free people generally do – generously. Call them a faction, and they become factious." Macdonald's relationship with French Canadians was not always happy, but he understood that Canada could not survive without accommodating French-speaking Canadians. We live with this issue today.

Other aspects of Macdonald's career are explained by another constant in Canadian history: the struggle for national unity. His greatest achievement, of course, was Confederation, which brought our provinces together. He then faced threats to the fragile unity of Confederation. These threats came from every region: British Columbia, the prairies, Ontario, Quebec, and the Maritimes. The problem of national unity has never been solved. We continue to wrestle with the problem and to make adjustment after adjustment. When we study Macdonald, we study problems that are forever current.

We are a small nation of people who live next to a great power. Throughout his life John A. Macdonald was concerned about that central fact of Canadian history. Can Canada survive in the face of the huge power to the south? Militarily the United States is vastly stronger than Canada. Economically we are overshadowed by the sheer magnitude of American enterprise. The dynamic nature of U.S. society has always attracted some of our brightest and most innovative people. Macdonald's concern was not that of a paranoid man. After all, the United States attacked Canada during the War of 1812, and allowed gangs of border raiders to invade the country in the 1830s and 1860s.

Confederation itself was at least in part a response to the American political-military threat. The National Policy of the late nineteenth century was designed to give us economic autonomy. We still live next to the United States, which is now one of the three strongest countries in the world. Our problems continue; Macdonald's concerns remain current.

Macdonald was a national figure who was forced to deal with problems that continue to plague Canada. This is enough to explain his importance. Perhaps, however, his sustained popularity rests as much on his humanity. He was no cold and calculating political technocrat. Sir John was warm and approachable; he was also defined by a tragic family life, and by intensely human flaws. He inspired love and loyalty in his followers, and he had time to care for them in spite of a first wife who was chronically ill and a daughter who lived as a quasi-invalid. Macdonald drank too much and dispensed favours and patronage in a manner that all too often smacked of corruption.

Today some say that Canada is at a crossroads. It is. But such has always been the case. By reading about Sir John A. Macdonald we should be able to learn something about what Canada was then – and is now. This book is an attempt to bring Macdonald to Canadians through illustrations that are explained in brief notes. The author's hope is that the flavour and excitement of nineteenth-century Canada become a little clearer to any reader who wants to understand his country. Canada cannot be understood without John A. Macdonald; he is everyman's Canadian.

Donald Swainson

Donald Swainson
November 23, 1978
Kingston, Ontario.

11

1891

The saddle was empty.
Sir John A. Macdonald was dead.

Canadians were shocked and stunned. Sir John A. had dominated Canada for over a generation. Now he was gone.

Even cartoonist John Wilson Bengough, a critic of Macdonald's, relented with this drawing when Macdonald died on June 6, 1891.

The country mourned its lost leader.

They gave him a funeral
appropriate to a man
who had presided over
the birth of his country.

Canadians filed by as he
lay in state in the Senate
Chamber in Ottawa.

Thousands of grieving

Even Nature seemed to underscore the drama of the occasion.

A journalist noted: "As the funeral car slowly passed the Parliament buildings, the forked lightnings played above the tower, and, with the echoing crash of thunder, torrents of rain came down drenching the processionists. It was the first thunderstorm of the season at the Capitol."

From St. Alban's, a draped train took his body to his boyhood town of Kingston. The funeral was ornate, with City Hall decorated in black and a long, official funeral procession.

More saddened Canadians awaited Sir John in Kingston.

The custom of the day
was to publish a
pamphlet listing the order
of the funeral procession.

RT. HON. SIR JOHN MACDONALD,
K.C.B., PREMIER,
DIED AT OTTAWA, JUNE 6, 1891,
INTERRED AT
CATARAQUI CEMETERY JUNE 11TH

The Order of Funeral from City Hall, Kingston

Kingston Firemen.
Masonic Order.
Gananoque Carriage Works Band.
Canton Kingston, I.O.O.F.
Cataraqui & Kingston Lodges, I.O.O.F.
Manchester Order of Odd-Fellows.
'Prentice Boys.
Orange Brethren.
Orange Young Britons.
Orange True Blues.
Independent Order Foresters.
Canadian Order Foresters.
Ancient Order Foresters.
Catholic Order Foresters.

St. Patrick's Society.
C. M. Ben. Ass'n.
Y. I. C. Ben. Ass'n.
A. O. United Workmen.
Select Knights.
Royal Arcanum.
St. Andrew's Society.
Sons of Scotland.
Sons of England.
St. George's Society.
Kingston Police.
4th Regiment Cavalry, 8 abreast.
Bands of Battery A and 14th P. W. O.
Rifles.
Battery A, 14 Battalion.
Royal Military College Cadets.
Clergy.
Funeral Director.
Flowers.
Pall Bearers.   Hearse.   Pall Bearers.
Mourners.
Governor-General and Staff.
Col. Gzowski representing Her Majesty
the Queen.
Her Majesty's Troops and Naval
Officers.

Lt.-Governors of Provinces and Staffs.
Archbishops and Bishops.
Members of Cabinet.
Speaker of Senate.
Chief Judges of Courts of Law and
Equity.
Members of Senate.
Speaker House of Commons.
Puisne Judges of Courts of Law and
Equity.
Members House of Commons.
Members Executive Councils of
Provinces.
Speakers of Legislative Councils and
Members.
Speakers of Legislative Assembly and
Members.
Consuls of Foreign Powers.
Deputy Ministers.
Law Societies.
Officers of Militia.
Mayor and Corporation of Kingston.
Deputations from Cities and Towns.
Citizens.
Carriages.

W. M. DRENNAN,   Funeral Director.

In Loving Memory

City Hall on the day of
Macdonald's funeral

The Prime Minister was buried in Cataraqui Cemetery beside his first wife, a simple cross marking his grave.

Macdonald had helped make Canada a transcontinental nation.

He had also affected the history of the British Empire.

In recognition of his contribution to imperial history, this statue was placed in St. Paul's Cathedral in London, England, after his death.

Macdonald was gone.

Canadian public life would never be the same. Even Wilfrid Laurier, Macdonald's political opponent and leader of the Liberal Party, recognized the terrible loss the country would feel.

He spoke for all Canadians when he said: "In fact the place of Sir John A. Macdonald in this country was so large and so absorbing that it is almost impossible to conceive that the politics of this country, the fate of this country, will continue without him."

His life ended in splendour.
His beginnings in Glasgow were far more modest.

On January 11, 1815, he was born into a Scottish family. His mother, Helen Shaw, was a Highlander; his father, Hugh Macdonald, a chronically unsuccessful businessman.

The family moved to Canada in 1820.

They settled in the Kingston area, where they had relatives. John spent his childhood at Hay Bay, on the Bay of Quinte, and later, in a stone house on Rideau Street, Kingston.

Macdonald's Rideau Street home

Macdonald decided on a career in law.

In 1836, Macdonald, only twenty-one years old, was admitted to the bar of Upper Canada. He became a very successful lawyer, and practised in a number of offices in Kingston.

In 1843, the people elected him to Kingston's City Council. It was the beginning of a political career that would last for forty-eight years.

25

At the beginning of his legal career, John A. was interested in whatever kind of case came his way.

He helped people buy property; he also assisted landlords who wished to evict tenants. The young lawyer represented mortgage holders who decided to foreclose on those who could no longer meet their payments.

Some of his biggest early cases involved spectacular crimes. In the fall of 1837, for example, he defended William Brass, who was accused of raping a young girl. The case was sensational and received a great deal of publicity; Macdonald's defence was energetic and clever, but not good enough. Brass was convicted and duly hanged in public.

Another famous case emerged from the Rebellion of 1837, when a minority of embittered Upper Canadians attempted to take the province out of the empire. The rebels were easily crushed, but their American sympathizers wanted to continue the struggle. Various U.S.-based groups resolved to invade Upper Canada

and liberate a people that they foolishly believed were oppressed. Nils von Schoultz led one of these groups. In November, 1838, his men landed on the north shore of the St. Lawrence River near Prescott. The invaders were defeated at the Battle of the Windmill; von Schoultz was captured. Sixteen Canadians had been killed, with sixty wounded, and a young Canadian lieutenant was killed and then mutilated. Needless to say, public opinion was aroused. Macdonald understood his region's opinion but agreed to defend von Schoultz, who was court-martialled. Von Schoultz had no real defence and was executed without much delay. Macdonald's work as a criminal lawyer might not have done much for his clients, but it helped gain for the aspiring lawyer a reputation as an articulate and courageous attorney. Over the long run, however, Macdonald gave up criminal law and concentrated on business activity. He speculated heavily in land himself, and became a very important corporation lawyer.

In 1843, his visit "home," as English-speaking Canadians then called Britain, was financed with the winnings from a card game called loo. Loo is a game of high risk, in which very large amounts of money can be won or lost. Years later Sir John described this marathon session: "In 1842, a lot of us sat down to play cards…We played loo, and I won everything. They then said that they must have their revenge. We played again, and I won. I am most unlucky, and this was a mere stroke of luck. I then said I will come back, but it must be for the last time, as I am leaving for England in a day or two. I came back and won the third time, nearly two thousand dollars in all, went home and had six months holiday on that money, and never played for money since."

For us in late twentieth century Canada, Macdonald's winnings would be the equivalent value of well over $20,000. Loo is still played in Kingston, and often by lawyers.

That same year, he married his cousin, Isabella Clark, a pretty girl he met while holidaying in his native Scotland.

The marriage was to be a great tragedy.

Isabella, or Isa as John called her, became ill a year after their marriage. An invalid until her death, she was often heavily sedated with opium.

Macdonald decided that Isabella needed the quiet of a country home.

In 1848, he rented **Bellevue**, a villa then just west of Kingston. It was a pretentious house, which provoked Macdonald to comment: "I have taken a cottage, or rather, I beg its pardon, a **Villa**...The House was built for a retired grocer, who was resolved to have a 'Eyetalian Willar,' and has built the most fantastic concern imaginable. From the previous laudable tho' rather prosaic pursuits of the worthy landlord the house is variously known in Kingston as Tea Caddy Castle, Molasses Hall and Muscovada Cottage."

Bellevue has been restored and is now a popular tourist site. It illustrates the lifestyle of a nineteenth-century professional family.

The kitchen

The study

A reconstructed gazebo on the grounds

Note the
elegance of the
dining room

Macdonald's own crib, on permanent loan to Bellevue House

Even during her thirteen years of agony Isabella gave birth to two sons.

John Alexander, Jr. was born in 1847 but died one year later. Hugh John, born in 1850, survived to follow his father's political footsteps.

He was to become the Member of Parliament for Winnipeg, Minister of the Interior and Premier of Manitoba.

These early years were not happy ones for Macdonald.

After 1844, he became M.P. for Kingston and was often away from home. Isabella's illness prevented any normal home life. One child had died in infancy; the other could not be brought up by an invalid mother and a harassed and often absent father.

He sought comfort in the company of political cronies, and began to drink heavily.

During his life, he would spend huge amounts of time with his friends in clubs and lounges. The Smoking Room of the House of Commons was also used for drinking.

One of Macdonald's intimates was John Rose.

He was a young Montrealer who would later become Finance Minister and a Father of Confederation.

Rose and Macdonald drank in bizarre fashion. Lord Carnarvon described one incident: "When quite a young man he and Sir John Rose, and a third, whose name I forget, went into the States and wandered about as strolling musicians. Macdonald played some rude instrument, Rose enacted the part of a bear and danced, and a third did something else. To the great amusement of themselves and everyone else, they collected pence by their performances in wayside taverns..."

John A. devoted himself to his political career and, in return, Kingstonians lavished support on their favourite son.

Court House in Kingston

In 1844 he won Kingston by 275 to 42 votes; in 1857 his poor opponent received seven votes to 1,189 for John A.

Macdonald appreciated this massive support and very carefully tended to the interests of Kingston. He gloated to Henry Smith, a close political colleague, in 1855: "As soon as the Court House is finished we will build a Customs House and Post Office, thus getting up three fine public buildings in old Kingston." To this day these remain three of Kingston's finest buildings.

Custom House

Post Office

Macdonald became a smash success in politics.

An effective spokesman in Parliament, he favourably impressed party leaders and was appointed Receiver General in 1847. In 1854, he emerged as a major Conservative leader and was appointed Prime Minister of the Province of Canada in 1857.

Union politics were volatile and exciting. Political warfare was never-ending. The key issues were separate schools, which were usually opposed by Protestants and supported by Catholics, transportation

policy, corruption in government, and trade relations with Britain and the United States.

Each section of the Union had the same number of M.P.P.s. After 1851, Upper Canada had more people than Lower Canada, and therefore demanded an end to equal representation. The cry was for representation by population, shortened to "Rep by Pop."

Race was also an issue; many people in Upper Canada were convinced that French Canadians had too much influence in the Union. The result was that a nasty form of anti-French racism entered Union politics. There were many other issues, of course, but the Union's main problems promoted division and hatred.

Union politics were lively and exciting, reflecting the strong personalities of party leaders.

John Hillyard
Cameron

John Carling

Macdonald's Conservative colleagues were a powerful group. George Etienne Cartier was the strongest Conservative in the history of French Canada, and Macdonald's most valuable ally.

John Hillyard Cameron represented Toronto Conservatism and was a rising power until he went bankrupt in the Panic of 1857.

John Carling led the Conservatives in western Ontario. A wealthy brewer, Carling was an important Tory for over fifty years. He was regarded as a handsome man, but the irreverent Macdonald countered that "no man could be as honest as John Carling looked."

Nineteenth century politics were crude and corrupt. Bribery, intimidation, influence peddling, manipulation of electoral machinery and violence were common. In the general election of 1857, for example, hundreds of fraudulent votes were cast in government ridings. The organizers were shameless. For their phony voters they used such names as George Washington, Julius Caesar and Judas Iscariot!

G. E. Cartier

Macdonald's fate would also be strongly tied to two former law associates from his Kingston days, Campbell and Mowat.

Oliver Mowat, Macdonald's first law student, chose an opposing political philosophy and became one of John A.'s most effective Liberal opponents.

At one point, these three close acquaintances simultaneously held three of Canada's most important posts:

☐ Macdonald was Prime Minister of Canada (1867-73; 1878-91)

☐ Campbell was Lieutenant-Governor of Ontario (1887-92)

☐ Mowat was Premier of Ontario (1872-96).

Mowat was known to his contemporaries as "the Christian statesman." He led a flawless private life. Such a man was not likely to be popular with John A. who, in a sarcastic moment, is reputed to have said: "One strong point I admire about Oliver Mowat is his handwriting."

Alexander Campbell had been Macdonald's second articled law student and later joined the firm as a partner. He worked behind the scenes running Macdonald's successful Kingston campaigns. In time, Campbell was appointed to several cabinet posts and became a Father of Confederation.

In the late 1840s, heated controversy arose over an idea called "Responsible Government."

Lord Elgin, Governor-General of Canada, agreed that the country be given a substantial amount of self-government. The Tories were furious, arguing that the change would lead to the breakup of the Empire. Moderate Conservatives like Macdonald made the transition and consequently dominated the Conservative Party during the 1850s and 60s.

But the union of French and English Canada was doomed to fail.

Ontario and Quebec found it impossible to operate within the stifling framework of a legislative union; there was also pressure to expand and build a transcontinental economy. George Brown, Canada's most powerful Reform politician and owner of the influential Toronto **Globe**, joined with other political allies to encourage the creation of a federal union with a strong government.

The Great Coalition, a government dominated by John A. Macdonald, George Etienne Cartier, and George Brown was formed in 1864. It was committed to the confederation of all British North America–from sea to sea.

They immediately contacted the four self-governing colonies of the Atlantic region.

The result was the crucially important Charlottetown Conference of 1864, where leaders of British North America agreed that a federal union of their self-governing colonies should be sought.

The four Atlantic Provinces resisted federation.

Two of them finally agreed to join the new union. Charles Tupper of Nova Scotia and Samuel Leonard Tilley of New Brunswick worked with Macdonald at Charlottetown and brought their provinces into the union. Without them, Confederation would have been impossible.

Tilley

As a reward for their work, Tupper and Tilley received a place in Macdonald's cabinets. They also led the Conservative Party in their respective provinces.

Encouraged by their success at Charlottetown, the leaders called another conference later in the year.

Representatives of Newfoundland, Prince Edward Island, Nova Scotia, New Brunswick and Canada met in Quebec City. During the Quebec Conference they worked out a detailed plan for confederation in a series of seventy-two resolutions.

When they were not at work, the Maritimers, with their wives and daughters, enjoyed an introduction to Canadian high society. Numerous balls and parties were provided in their honour.

The Founder's of Confederation Of The DOMINION of CANADA
Photos Taken During Quebec Conference (Oct 10-28 - 1864)

Souvenir Group of Confederation Jubilee (1917)

Delegates to the Quebec Conference

South of the border, an ugly war was raging.

The conflict would have a strong effect on Canada's struggle for confederation. On April 12, 1861 southern guns began bombarding Fort Sumter. Until 1865 the American North and South would be locked in conflict as bloody as it was bitter.

How did Canadians react? Many political leaders were sure that a stronger central government in the States would have prevented a Civil War. This convinced the Fathers of Confederation that **our** federal government should be very strong. Confederation was thus designed with Ottawa stronger than the provinces.

Canadians were terrified of American military strength.

Army teamsters

During the Civil War the North and South became the strongest military powers in the western world. As long as they were fighting each other, Canada was in no danger. But once it became clear that the North was going to win, Canada was in very serious trouble. Several Canadian leaders, with John A. Macdonald among them, had sympathized with the South. So had many British leaders. It was feared that the North would retaliate by invading Canada.

Another fear was that the North might not restrain the Fenians, a secret brotherhood of Irish terrorists who sought to attack Canada. These Irish-Americans supported Irish nationalism and wanted an Ireland independent of Britain. Although they could not reach Britain, Canada was close enough to attack; this would hurt Britain. The Fenian movement, although disorganized, was potentially dangerous, and included many veterans of the Northern armies. There were several Fenian border raids between 1866 and 1871. The most serious was near Niagara Falls in 1866, in which nine Canadians were killed.

Lincoln, McClellan and officers
at Army of Potomac
Headquarters

The threat from the United States was exaggerated, but Canadian fears were nonetheless real.

The result was a strengthening of the confederation movement. A united Canada, including the Maritimes and the West, would be a stronger Canada. These threats also intensified Canadian loyalty; that, too, worked to the advantage of confederation.

One Father of Confederation was acutely aware of the American threat.

Thomas D'Arcy McGee, the leader of Canada's Irish Catholics, was a temperamental leader, but a highly gifted orator. He occupied an important place in Canadian politics until 1868, when he was assassinated by a Fenian sympathizer.

In strong language, McGee warned Canadians of the danger from the United States in his speech in the Confederation Debates of 1865:

"The policy of our neighbours to the south of us has always been aggressive. There has always been a desire amongst them for the acquisition of new territory...They coveted Florida, and seized it; they coveted Louisiana, and purchased it; they coveted Texas, and stole it; and then they picked a quarrel with Mexico, which ended by their getting California...The acquisition of Canada was the first ambition of the American Confederacy, and never ceased to be so, when her troops were a handful and her navy scarce a squadron. Is it likely to be stopped now, when she counts her guns afloat by thousands and her troops by hundreds of thousands?"

Tuponian or Hochelagander?

McGee was not always serious. In the same debate he had some fun with the outrageous names that some had proposed for a new federation:

"One individual chooses Tuponia and another Hochelaga, as a suitable name for the new nationality. Now I would ask any honourable member of this House how he would feel if he woke up some fine morning and found himself, instead of a Canadian, a Tuponian or a Hochelagander?"

Good sense prevailed and the new federation was styled "one Dominion under the name of Canada."

Samuel Leonard Tilley, a religious man, was probably responsible for part of our country's name. It comes from the 72nd Psalm: "May he have dominion from sea to sea, and from the River to the ends of the earth!"

Finally, in 1866, Canada was about to become a Confederation.

Representatives of Nova Scotia, New Brunswick and Canada met at the Westminster Palace Hotel in London to prepare the final resolutions.

Macdonald was elected chairman of the London Conference in

recognition of his importance to the confederation movement. What emerged from the conference was a constitution called the British North America Act, which can still be amended only by the British Parliament.

When it was passed by Parliament in 1867, one of Macdonald's greatest hopes was realized.

Although Confederation was not immediately popular throughout Canada, it was a success in Kingston.

A large crowd gathered in Market Square on July 1, 1867 to hear the reading of the proclamation announcing the birth of the Dominion of Canada.

Canada was now a nation. People began to realize that Confederation was a great event.

The Great Seal
of Canada

Needless to say, the politicians argued over who was the real Father of Confederation. Liberals favoured George Brown. Conservatives knew in their hearts that John A. Macdonald was the father of his country.

Confederation changed Macdonald's life.

Before 1867 he was one of the most important politicians in what was to become Ontario. After 1867 he was the most important political leader in Canada. It was logical to appoint him Prime Minister of Canada and charge him with the task of forming Canada's first government.

Macdonald's achievement was marked in another way. On Dominion Day, 1867, Canadians learned that their Prime Minister had been knighted; he was now Prime Minister **Sir** John A. Macdonald.

John A. Macdonald had a sure touch when he dealt with ordinary people, and he was able to inspire profound loyalty in his followers.

In 1866 he illustrated these talents while visiting the lumbering village on Garden Island, near Kingston. Anthony Malone told the story in his **Reminiscences**, which have never been published.

"Somewhere about the year 1866 John A. Macdonald paid a visit to Garden Island. Whilst [there] he espied an aged Irishman...Turning to me, Sir John asked, 'Who is that old man over there?' to which I replied 'John Dignem.'

'Have I ever seen him before? Do you know if he ever attended any of my political meetings?'

'Yes,' I replied, 'he was at one of your meetings in the City Hall, Kingston a few years ago when we all went over to hear you.'

Sir John went at once to the man, extended his hand remarking, 'Why, is this my old friend Dignem? How are you, I have not seen you since that night you were at my meeting in the City Hall some years ago–how have you been ever since?'

Lowering his voice to almost a whisper he continued; his mouth being close to Dignem's ear, 'You stood by me nobly that evening and I am proud of you.'

Dignem was thunderstruck and ran around amongst the men remarking 'Did yez iver see the loiks av that. The gentleman knowed me and he niver sot eyes on me but onct afore...[If] I iver had a boy vote agin that gintleman I'd break his back.'"

Ottawa was named the capital.

In 1865, it had been named the capital of the Province of Canada. Now the British North America Act confirmed it as capital of the Dominion of Canada.

Life for Union politicians was complicated by the fact that there was never a stable capital during this period. It moved constantly, as follows:

Kingston, 1841-44
Montreal, 1844-49
Toronto, 1849-51
Quebec, 1851-55
Toronto, 1855-59
Quebec, 1859-65
Ottawa, 1865-67.

In twenty-six years the capital of the Province of Canada had seven locations in five cities. The capital was moved six times; the result was substantial confusion for civil servants and an unusually unsettled existence for politicians.

After Confederation, Macdonald's life revolved around Ottawa.

Here Macdonald would make his home for the rest of his life. With only 20,000 inhabitants, Ottawa was an unsophisticated and isolated town with an unattractive climate. The famous journalist Goldwin Smith caustically noted: "Ottawa is a sub-arctic lumber-village converted by royal mandate into a political cockpit."

Ottawa and her sister city, Hull, Quebec, separated by the Ottawa River, were frontier lumbering communities. Lumber was their business; logs, their bread and butter.

The Rideau Canal, which
connects Kingston with Ottawa,
was one of the attractive
features of the town. It provided
a variety of scenic views.

In summer, the Rideau provided the most prosaic of settings.

In winter, the results could be dramatic.

One of the first priorities of the new government was to complete the Houses of Parliament.

But the construction of the Parliament buildings became controversial and scandalous. The initial contracts for the Parliament Building and the two departmental buildings involved $688,505 in costs. By Dominion Day, 1867, $2,572,193.24 had been spent. That inflated sum did not include a roof over the main tower. Nor, in the original plans, was provision made for heating.

The main contract went to a political supporter of the government despite the fact that his tender included no schedule of prices. During 1860, although most of the original estimate was spent, the buildings were not yet above ground.

When finished, however, the results were spectacular, and contrasted vividly with the surrounding shanty town.

Construction of the library

Parliament Buildings with
shanty town in foreground

73

Despite all the problems involved, the completed Parliament buildings were the finest public buildings in Canada.

Macdonald's adopted city later honoured him with the Sir John A. Macdonald monument.

Meanwhile, a major event occurred in John A.'s private life which would affect his career as well.

During the winter of 1867, while at the London Conference, he accidentally encountered Susan Agnes Bernard on Bond Street. He had met her casually before; she was a sister of one of his aides. Agnes, as she was usually called, "possessed a keen wit, a quick perception, a liberal mind and a certain unselfishness of heart." She was "brilliant …in conversation, and had no small degree of literary taste and talent…"

After a whirlwind courtship, they were married in London on February 16, 1867. This second marriage for Macdonald involved a major break with the past. Agnes had never lived in Kingston and never would. Ottawa was their home.

"Home" began to have a new meaning for Macdonald.

Lady Macdonald, elegant, cultured and interested in society, gave Sir John A. his first secure home life since the early days of his first marriage. Agnes, twenty-one years younger than her husband, was filled with energy and gaiety. She liked to meet and entertain his colleagues and cronies. Macdonald began to enjoy his strangely settled new life.

Lady Macdonald loved to work with her husband in every area. They learned the sign language used by those who cannot talk, and she would thus communicate with Sir John when she was in the gallery of the House of Commons.

Earnscliffe became home for Lady Macdonald and Sir John A.

The Macdonalds moved into Earnscliffe, the Eagle's Cliff, in 1870, although they did not buy it until 1882.

Sir John A. spent a great deal of his time at Earnscliffe, where he worked in a spacious and cluttered study.

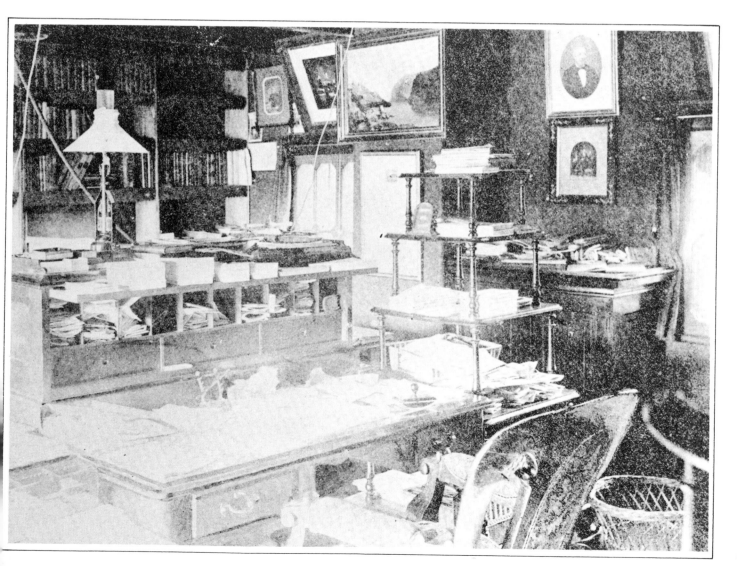

As he began to settle comfortably into the roles of senior statesman and family man, he decided to adopt a coat of arms.

John A. Macdonald.

But tragedy struck again.

On February 8, 1869, Agnes gave birth to a beautiful daughter, Mary. They soon learned that she was not normal—"a victim of hydrocephalus—an affliction caused by an effusion of water on the brain."

She would be a semi-invalid all her life.

Lady Agnes and Sir John were grief-stricken, but they loved and protected their daughter. Macdonald was devoted to Mary, and wrote brief letters to her when they were separated.

"You remember that Mamma cut my hair and made me look like a cropped donkey," he told her in 1873. "It has grown quite long again. When you come home, you must not pull it too hard. I intend to have new stories for you when you come in the morning into Papa's bed and cuddle him up."

Mary learned to write and kept her father informed. For some reason, she called her mother by her given name. When she was eight she wrote to her father as follows:

"Dear Father, when are you coming back? I hope you will be back soon for Agnes misses you very much and says often to me, 'how I wish my husband was back.' The house seems so dull and lonely without you and I miss my evening stories very much."

Mary's illness was but the latest in a chain of unhappy events in John A.'s private life.

His first wife had died young, after terrible suffering. His first son died in infancy. He hardly knew his other son, and their relationship was often stormy and unpleasant. Now, his only daughter was suffering from a debilitating disease.

It is a marvel that Sir John was able to weather these tragedies and function as a creative statesman.

A quiet place at Earnscliffe showing Mary's wheelchair

Macdonald's domestic tragedies, however, did not lessen his success as a statesman.

During his first government (1867-73) he proved himself a shrewd politician. His first spectacular coup was engineering the appointment of John Sandfield Macdonald–a renegade Liberal now working with John A.–as Premier of Ontario. This came as a shock to such Liberals as George Brown, who had expected to take power in Toronto and had hoped for the appointment of one of his associates.

Sandfield Macdonald was a blunt man. When a group from Strathroy, Ontario asked for a political favour, he replied: "What the hell has Strathroy done for me?"

How could Sandfield Macdonald become Ontario's Premier?

Thanks to an unusual aspect of the Canadian constitution, when a new political entity is established, the Premier or Prime Minister is appointed **before** an election is held.

In this way, Governor-General Monck appointed John A. Macdonald Prime Minister of Canada before the new federation legally existed. Macdonald then appointed Sir Henry William Stisted as Lieutenant-Governor of Ontario, and urged him to make John Sandfield Macdonald (no relation) Ontario's first Premier.

When the first Ontario and federal elections were finally held, the two Macdonalds were safely in power and could exert strong pressure on the Ontario electorate.

A disgruntled George Brown described Stisted as "an old fool" when he heard of his impending appointment as Lieutenant-Governor. Perhaps Brown felt differently when he woke up on Dominion Day, 1867, and realized that H.W. Stisted and John A. Macdonald had denied the Liberals the government of Ontario.

From the very beginning, Canada's hopes for a strong federation of provinces were plagued by delays and disappointments.

Nova Scotia had been unwillingly brought into Confederation by Charles Tupper, premier of the province. He had refused to take the issue to the people, but when the election of 1867 was held, there was little doubt where they stood. Joseph Howe and his anti-confederationists swept Nova Scotia federally and provincially. Tupper was the only pro-confederationist elected to Ottawa. Nova Scotia's position in the union was tenuous at best.

Tupper

Furthermore, the vast territories west of Ontario had yet to be acquired.

In 1869, Canada purchased the Hudson's Bay Company's lands, encompassing what is now Manitoba, Saskatchewan, Alberta and parts of northern Ontario, northern Quebec and the North-West Territories. In return, the Hudson's Bay Company received 300,000 pounds, 50,000 acres adjoining its trading posts, and 5% of the fertile lands on the prairies.

The business deal itself was impressive: indeed, Canada had carried out one of the largest real estate transactions in world history.

Red River carts leaving Fort
Garry

But a costly error was made with the appointment of William McDougall.

He was named first Lieutenant-Governor of the area designated as the North-West Territories. McDougall, once valuable to Macdonald as an Upper Canada Liberal who had supported Confederation, was no longer useful as a cabinet minister in Macdonald's government. Liberals had begun returning to support George Brown, and McDougall had lost his political influence in Ontario. Macdonald saw the appointing of McDougall as Lieutenant-Governor a convenient way to remove him from the cabinet. The consequences were disastrous.

McDougall, a racist who despised the Indians and mixed-blood Métis who inhabited the prairies, clashed with the native people. They were already furious because they had not been consulted about the transfer of their land, and were determined to retain their cultural integrity. McDougall's racist atti-tudes only inflamed these proud people further. Conflict was inevitable.

In the midst of this turmoil, a leader arose—one who would defend his people's homeland and achieve a decisive place in Canadian history.

His name was Louis Riel.

Riel was a Métis, a person of mixed Indian and white blood; his mother tongue was French and he was a Roman Catholic. Born in 1844, he received an excellent education in Montreal and then returned to his beloved prairies.

His father, Louis Riel the elder, had been a leader of the Métis. It was natural that 25-year-old Louis, well educated and the son of a powerful man, should assume leadership.

A good organizer and a superb orator, he had learned much in Montreal about central Canadian politics. He knew that many Canadians feared the United States and its possible annexation of Canada's North-West. That alternative future gave him a bargaining point.

In reality, however, Riel wanted no union with the United States. He knew his people, their language and their religion would be better protected within Canada. Riel's real objective was to force Canada to negotiate with the Métis on the terms upon which the West would enter Confederation. Like most prairie premiers ever since, Riel was a western nationalist. He distrusted Ontario and wanted the interests of his region protected.

Riel and his associates refused to let William McDougall enter their territory.

Hon. William McDougall, Minister of Public Works

Riel and his council

Permission to enter would have been recognition of Canadian authority. McDougall, defeated, languished awhile in the United States near Manitoba, and then went back to Ontario in disgrace.

The Métis occupied Fort Garry.

This Hudson's Bay Company fort was the strongest place on the prairies; it was the strategic key to the West. During the winter of 1869-70 it was Riel's headquarters and the capital of the Métis nation.

That winter, Thomas Scott was executed.

An Orangeman and racist who had been captured by the Métis, he was court-martialled and sentenced to death after he insulted and abused his Métis guards. He faced a firing squad on March 4, 1870.

The execution of Scott was a serious blunder on Riel's part. The Métis were French-speaking; Scott spoke English. Racial animosities in central Canada were stirred up as English Canadians demanded revenge for Scott, while French Canadians defended the Métis and their desire to protect their religion and language.

Riel and the Métis finally succeeded in negotiating the entry of the West into Confederation. As a result, the Province of Manitoba was established in 1870, with guarantees for the French language and Catholic education.

Years later Riel commented, "I know that through the grace of God I am the founder of Manitoba."

The first Riel Rebellion was over, but the political issues it raised remained alive.

Many English Canadians wanted Riel tried for the execution of Thomas Scott; French Canadians argued that Riel was being persecuted because he defended his culture. The debate became bitter. Macdonald sought to solve this political problem by avoiding it. He pretended that an attempt was being made to apprehend Riel; meanwhile, he was paying Riel out of his government's secret service fund to remain in hiding.

A CASE OF RIEL DISTRESS!

Mearcy! but I'd like fine to arrest them both.

I wish I could catch the Scoundrel –I do– so help me G...rits!!

Back in the East, labour troubles began to surface.

Trade unionism loomed as a sensitive issue in 1872 when the Toronto **Globe's** typographical union went on strike. Macdonald saw an opportunity to steal a march on his old opponent, George Brown, and introduced legislation that strengthened the unions' position. As he had hoped, Macdonald emerged as the "friend of the working man." A group of trade unionists responded by presenting Lady Macdonald with a golden casket. Macdonald thanked the working men on Agnes' behalf and noted:

"I am a working man myself. I know that I work more than nine hours every day myself; and then I think that I am a practical mechanic. If you look at the Confederation Act, in the framing of which I had some hand, you will admit that I am a pretty good joiner; and, as for cabinet-making, I have had as much experience as Jacques and Hay* themselves."

The crowd loved it.

*well-known Toronto cabinet-makers of the day

It was an election year and Macdonald needed all the friends he could get.

1872. It was a tough election, which Macdonald won–but barely. The real trouble came after the electoral struggle was over. The source–the proposed transcontinental railroad.

In 1871, British Columbia had joined the union on the condition that she would have a rail link with central Canada. Sir Hugh Allan, a wealthy Montreal business tycoon, wanted the contract to build the line. He lobbied hard for it, and during the election donated $179,000 to various Conservative politicians. Allan received the contract, and agreed to construct a railroad to the Pacific. In return, his firm, the Canadian Pacific Railway Company, would receive substantial government subsidies, including $30,000,000 and 50,000,000 acres of land. Many people argued

Sir Hugh Allan

that Allan had bought the contract in return for his political donations. Thus began the makings of the Pacific Scandal, perhaps the most important government scandal in Canadian history.

Macdonald became entangled with Allan's vast wealth.
He began borrowing heavily from him.

In a fit of indiscretion, he wired Allan's lawyer, Conservative M.P. John Joseph Caldwell Abbott: "I must have another ten thousand; will be the last time of calling; do not fail me; answer today."
Abbott replied:
   "Draw on me for ten thousand dollars."
Abbott's law office in Montreal contained a mass of such incriminatory documents.

An ultimate political horror took place. Abbott's office was robbed.

The evidence fell into the hands of Lucius Seth Huntington, Liberal M.P. for Shefford, who broke the scandal in the House of Commons.

On April 2, 1873, Macdonald and his cabinet were accused of giving Sir Hugh Allan the Pacific Railway contract in return for his donations in 1872.

A vicious political struggle ensued.

Policeman G.B. "Nothing in it!
Then why not vindicate yourself
by having it thoroughly
examined.

I admit I with it.
took the Is there
money, anything
and wrong
bribed the about
electors that?

CHILLY SHORE OF OPPOSITION

TRYING TO SMUGGLE ACROSS.

POLICEMAN G. B. "NOTHING IN IT! THEN WHY NOT VINDICATE YOURSELF BY HAVING IT THOROUGHLY EXAMINED."

"WE IN CANADA SEEM TO HAVE LOST ALL IDEA OF JUSTICE, HONOR AND INTEGRITY."—THE MAIL, 26TH SEPTEMBER.

The Liberals wanted to bring down the government and destroy Macdonald's political career. Newspaper writers and cartoonists had a field day. Sir John A. did not fare well in the press.

Bribery was a regular part of the electoral process. Some years later Mr. Justice J.D. Armour put it succinctly when he said: "Is not bribery the corner-stone of Party Government?"

THE ELECTION MONSTER.

Some of John A.'s followers began to waver in their support.

Conservative leaders tried desperately to maintain support in the House of Commons, and much strategy was planned in the Council Chamber. Some members actually did desert the government.

The Government was in desperate trouble.

But Macdonald's instinct, when in difficulty, was to delay problems. His nickname, "Old Tomorrow," was well earned. He played for time by getting John Hillyard Cameron elected to chair a parliamentary committee to investigate Huntington's charges.

Cameron was hardly an objective observer: he was one of Macdonald's hacks, and had even obtained $5,000 from Sir Hugh Allan for support during the 1872 election.

J. H. Cameron

The Council Chamber

Macdonald's Government was finished.

WHITHER ARE WE DRIFTING?

The Pacific Scandal crisis shattered the country's confidence in its leaders. "Old Tomorrow" worked valiantly to prevent an early reconvening of Parliament in 1873, but delaying tactics simply postponed the inevitable.

His next step was to offer his resignation to Lord Dufferin, the British aristocrat who had been Governor-General since 1872. Although Dufferin had been under great pressure from the Liberals to dismiss Macdonald during the crisis, he insisted that political decisions concerning Canada be made by Canadians.

Dufferin explained: "I suppose I am the only person in the Dominion whose faith in the wisdom and in the infallibility of Parliament is never shaken. Each of you, gentlemen, only believes your wishes and convictions. I, gentlemen, believe in Parliament, no matter which way it votes, and to those men alone whom the absolute will of the Confederated Parliament of the Dominion may assign me as my responsible advisers, can I give my confidence."

On November 5, 1873, Macdonald went to Dufferin and resigned as Canada's first Prime Minister.

Macdonald was not the only victim of the Pacific Scandal. Another major casualty was Sir George Etienne Cartier, his co-leader.

Cartier's own political vulnerability caused him to accept large donations from Allan to finance his personal re-election campaign. Nonetheless, he lost his seat.

During the entire campaign he was ill with Bright's disease. Although he sought medical assistance in England, he died there in 1873–ill and unhappy. Macdonald never found a political partner to replace him.

How could Macdonald have made the terrible errors of 1872-73?

Drink was known to be a very substantial factor in his erratic behaviour. Shortly after the fall of the government, Alexander Campbell, Macdonald's colleague, friend and former law partner explained the problem to a mutual friend.

"From the time he left Kingston, after his own election," explained the omnipresent Campbell, **"I am very much afraid that he kept himself more or less under the influence of wine, and that he really has no clear recollection of what he did on many occasions at Toronto and elsewhere after that period...I am very sorry to say that the same reason which impeded his management of the elections was operating during the whole of the days that Parliament remained in Session, and we never had the full advantage either of his abilities and judgment or of his nerve and courage. A night of excess always leaves a morning of nervous incapacity and we were subjected to this pain amongst others."**

Macdonald was out.

The new Prime Minister was Alexander Mackenzie, a dour Scotsman who led the Liberal Party. Mackenzie was honest, but plodding and dull.

Goldwin Smith, an unusually caustic journalist, said of Mackenzie: "If his strong point was having been a stonemason, his weak point was being a stone-mason still."

Ironically, years earlier, the new Prime Minister had unsuccessfully tendered for a contract to build a portion of the Parliament buildings that he now inhabited.

The Canadian people had lost more than their leadership. They had also lost their railroad.

As a result of the political disaster, Sir Hugh Allan's railway company could not raise enough money to build the transcontinental railroad. It was forced to give up its charter.

The new Liberal Government under Mackenzie had its share of problems. Most serious were weak leadership and the growing spectre of an economic depression.

The most brilliant man in Liberal politics was Edward Blake, who had led his party to victory in the Ontario election in 1871. After brief service as Premier of Ontario, he resigned in order to devote his full attention to federal politics.

Blake, however, was an erratic man, and he turned down the federal Liberal leadership in 1873. He found it impossible to work as a lieutenant to a Prime Minister less able than himself. Edward Blake was a main cause of the instability that plagued Mackenzie's ill-fated regime.

Another key figure in the Liberal Party was Richard Cartwright, a prominent member of a wealthy Kingston family.

Cartwright started his political career in 1863 as a Conservative M.P. He broke with Macdonald over several issues, but the Pacific Scandal played a major role in his decision to join the Liberal Party.

Cartwright was Minister of Finance from 1873-78. He was confronted by an economic depression that was serious by the mid-1870's. The Liberals had no solution to the Depression; Cartwright and his colleagues looked weak and ineffective.

The Depression contributed to other problems.

Mackenzie did not believe that Canada could afford to proceed with the rapid construction of the Pacific railway. Needless to say, British Columbia was angry over the delay.

XIV.—No. 9.   MONTREAL, SATURDAY, SEPTEMBER 9, 1876.   SINGLE COPIES, TEN CE. / $4 PER YEAR IN ADVA

BRITISH COLUMBIA IN A PET.

Meanwhile, Sir John had resumed the practice of law after his government fell in 1873.

He now had the time for this career, and needed the money. In 1875, he moved his family to Toronto. They lived in a pleasant house on Sherbourne Street.

Macdonald also lived for a time in this house on St. George Street

In 1874, a new leader emerged for the Liberals – one who was destined for a stunning political career.

As a result of the dismal Mackenzie years, Wilfrid Laurier appeared on the scene as a leader of the Liberal Party. He was first elected to the House of Commons in 1874 and entered the government in 1877.

This was the beginning of a political career that would span over thirty-five years. He would later serve as Canada's Prime Minister for fifteen of them, from 1896–1911.

Incredibly, John A. Macdonald survived the Pacific Scandal.

According to all political logic he should have been destroyed, but his party remained loyal and determined to overcome the disgrace of 1873.

The Liberals were not faring well. Political ineptitude and the economic crisis weakened the cabinet. Mackenzie and his colleagues were divided, and thus could not lead a united party. Several ministers were inexperienced and failed to develop the skills needed as federal cabinet ministers.

Macdonald knew how to exploit Liberal weakness.

That's the sort of a picnic I hanker after, Charlie! When will we have one like that?

THE ONLY SATISFYING PICNIC, AFTER ALL.

By 1876 he was on the offensive. The economy was in trouble, he pointed out. To correct this, he promised to introduce the National Policy, a programme of high tariffs which would protect our infant industries and give Canada an opportunity to build an industrial sector. It was a far better alternative than to supply raw materials to England and the United States and later buy back the manufactured goods from them. Why not manufacture such goods here, argued Sir John.

He began to spread his message by a pleasant medium—the political picnic. Opponents ridiculed Macdonald and his picnics, but they were devastatingly successful.

He won the election of 1878 with the slogan, "Canada for the Canadians."

Macdonald was indeed "The Great Political Conjurer." His key issue was the National Policy; he promised to raise tariffs to protect Canadian industry, but kept the policy vague in order not to alienate the free traders in the Maritimes.

THE GREAT POLITICAL CONJURER.
"ALL SORTS OF WINE POURED OUT OF ONE AND THE SAME BOTTLE."

Macdonald had fun with his audiences, who loved his more outrageous claims. Shortly after he returned to power in 1878 he explained the impact of his new government and of the National Policy.

"Trade revived, crops were abundant, and bank stocks once more became buoyant, owing to the confidence of the people of Canada in the new Administration.

"A citizen of Toronto assured me," continued Sir John with a straight face, "that his Conservative cow gave three quarts of milk more a day after the election than before; while a good Conservative lady friend solemnly affirmed that her hens laid more eggs, larger eggs, fresher eggs and more to the dozen ever since the new Administration came in."

The National Policy became a reality.

The National Policy, it was promised, would cure many of our problems. Even the horses would be healthier.

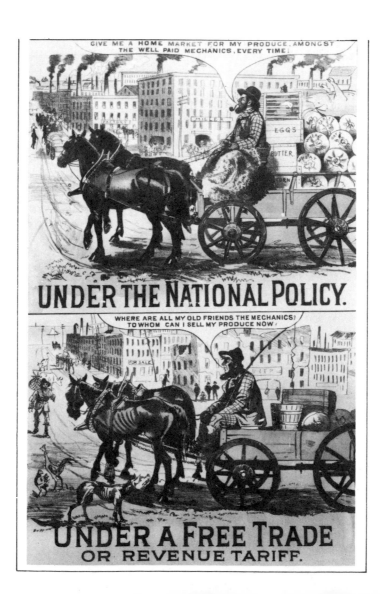

Protection would save the domestic economy for Canadians.

The N.P., as the National Policy came to be called, strongly appealed to Canada's profound suspicion of the United States. Americans, it was implied, would no longer be able to take our profits and use us as a dumping ground for excess goods.

It was put into effect through a series of budgets which raised tariffs in key areas such as farm implements, boots, and other manufacturing industries.

Dealing with British Columbia remained a problem.

There was bitterness over the delay of the promised Pacific railway due to the Depression. Sir John worked to pacify the "Cinderella of Confederation" but he knew that the only solution was to complete the transcontinental railroad.

With astonishing speed, the proposed railway became a reality.

A private firm, the Canadian Pacific Railway Company, was duly chartered to build the line. This company, one of the most important firms in Canadian history, was controlled by a group of businessmen and financiers with close links to the Bank of Montreal.

The contract required the CPR to complete the line by 1891.

In return, the company was given $38,000,000 worth of line already built by the government, 25 million acres of land, and $25,000,000.

The massive undertaking was completed with amazing speed. On November 7, 1885, Donald Smith, a member of the board of the CPR and later president of the Bank of Montreal, drove the last spike at Craigellachie.

Ironically, this same man had once been a political opponent of Macdonald's. Only seven years before he had provoked him into screaming in rage in the House of Commons: "That fellow Smith is the biggest liar I ever met."

As Macdonald physically attacked Smith, the Tory leader said: "I can lick you quicker than Hell can scorch a feather."

The construction of the CPR had been the largest building project in Canadian history. Thousands of workers, some of whom were Chinese, were employed.

In 1886, Sir John and his wife took their first train trip on the coveted railway.

After paying a brief visit to Port Arthur, they proceeded on to British Columbia. While there, they did the usual things tourists do. They visited glaciers, stared in awe at the mountains, and walked along Pacific beaches.

They also visited Government House.

When the first CPR transcontinental train arrived in Vancouver on May 23, 1887, the track had already been well used.

Macdonald was now at the height of his political career.

The early years of his government were productive and pleasant. The economy had improved and the government was creative. Macdonald easily controlled the House of Commons.

He was indeed "The Head of the Country."

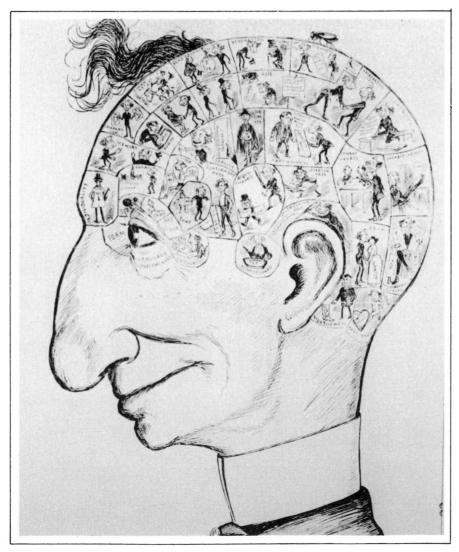

John Wilson Bengough's cartoon reflects the popular nineteenth century interest in phrenology–the science of studying character by observing the shape of the skull.

Perhaps the Macdonalds were a bit too confident.

There was a tinge of the ridiculous about Lady Macdonald being photographed in regal costume, and Sir John being sculpted in the style of an ancient Roman.

Macdonald's confidence was well-earned after 1878. But, as the 1880s progressed, he had reason to become depressed and worried.

The country was passing through a series of trials. First, there was a leadership problem. The cabinet as a whole was old and weak, and Macdonald had little assistance from the Ontario section.

However, two invaluable Nova Scotians were able to offer him substantial assistance. Charles Tupper, a political warhorse who had worked with Macdonald since Charlottetown in 1864, supervised the construction of the CPR.

In 1885, John Sparrow David Thompson left a career as judge to assist him in Ottawa. Both men would become Prime Ministers in the 1890s.

In the midst of internal disorder, the Government had to face the threat of a second rebellion in the West.

This weakened and divided government was in no condition to handle another rebellion in Western Canada.

Upper: Soldiers' graves, Battleford, Saskatchewan
Lower: Sewing corpses into canvas in preparation for burial, Fish Creek, North West Territories

Since the end of the Resistance of 1869-70, Louis Riel, a wanted man, had been forced to live in exile in the United States.

He suffered severe mental problems, and for a time was confined to an asylum. In 1884, while teaching school in Montana, a group of settlers from North Saskatchewan River area asked him to return and lead them in an agitation for better treatment from the Ottawa government. Riel agreed, and was very soon on the road to a second rebellion.

Fighting broke out in the Saskatchewan country between the Métis and the North-West Mounted Police. Shortly thereafter, Eastern Canadian and Manitoban militia men joined the Mounties in their struggle to suppress the Métis. Many Canadians were furious at the death and destruction that resulted.

Government troops rushed west over the nearly completed CPR and easily crushed the rising.

Riel was captured and taken to Regina to face trial for treason. The charge was grim:

"That Louis Riel, being a subject of our Lady the Queen, not regarding the duty of his allegiance, nor having the fear of God in his heart, but being moved and seduced by the instigation of the devil as a false traitor against our said Lady the Queen..."

Street scene in Regina at the time of the Riel trial

Regina was a crude fron-
tier town. Until the CPR
came through it was
named Pile of Bones.
Needless to say, facilities
in Regina were makeshift.

The shack in which Louis Riel
took his meals during the trial

A six-man jury found Riel guilty as charged. He was sentenced to be hanged.

Now the Government faced a terrible dilemma. French Canada did not want Riel hanged.

After all, they reasoned, he was almost certainly mentally ill and his Métis followers did have many legitimate grievances.

Wilfrid Laurier sympathized with the Métis rebellion: "Had I been born on the banks of the Saskatchewan, I would myself have shouldered a musket to fight against the neglect of governments and the shameless greed of speculators."

English Canadians, however, were often vicious in their condemnation of Riel. **The Toronto News** spoke for many when it thundered, "Strangle Riel with the French flag! That is the only use that rag can have in this country."

Macdonald and his government had to decide whether to spare

A RIEL UGLY POSITION.

Riel or let him hang. Either decision would infuriate many Canadians. As J.W. Bengough put it, the government was in "A Riel Ugly Position."

The Government chose death.

Once decided, Sir John became vehement. In a most unfortunate moment he remarked, "He shall hang though every dog in Quebec bark in his favour."

Louis Riel was executed on November 16, 1885. The result was catastrophic for Canada and the Conservative Party.

Edward Blake, who led the federal Liberals from 1880-87, used the Riel crisis to bolster Liberal strength. Although he had no desire to weaken the Liberals in English Canada, he clearly wanted to weaken Conservatives everywhere and give the Liberals a much needed boost in Quebec. Blake's strategy was to blame Macdonald's government for the crisis of 1885, not to defend Riel.

"Had there been no neglect, there would have been no rebellion," he explained. "If no rebellion, then no arrest. If no arrest, then no trial. If no trial, then no condemnation. If no condemnation, then no execution. They...who are responsible for the first are responsible for every link in that fatal chain."

Blake's position was damaging to Macdonald but, over the long run, Honoré Mercier was a far more dangerous man.

He kindled French-Canadian nationalism and used the scaffold from which Riel was hanged as a political platform.

"In killing Riel, Sir John not only struck our race at the heart, but struck the cause of justice and humanity..."

Mercier became Premier of an inflamed Quebec in 1887. To this day, Canada has lived with the results of a vibrant and aggressive French-Canadian nationalism.

Controversy over trade policies continued to plague the Government.

The N.P. had imposed high tariffs on many goods, which worked well during the prosperous days following the 1878 election. But during the early 1880s, hard times returned to Canada. Many people left the country to move to the States.

Liberal leaders, led by Sir Richard Cartwright, blamed the government and its National Policy, saying: "The Dominion that had begun in Lamentations seems to be ending in Exodus."

III.—No. 10.   MONTREAL, SATURDAY, MARCH 5, 1881.   [SINGLE COPIES, TEN CENTS. $4 PER YEAR IN ADVANCE.

U.S. BOUNDARY LINE

TREMENDOUS EXODUS OF CANADIANS 94,000 IN ONE YEAR

HOW THEY RECKON THE EXODUS.

B—CH—RD C—RTWR—GHT:—Another Canadian leaving the country, you perceive in this the effect of the suicidal policy of the Government.
L—N—RD T—LL—Y:—Here I say, you know, this fellow must have come in at the other gate.
BL—KE (At the other gate):—This way round gentlemen. If we can only get a few more of you to pass through we shall soon run the exodus up to a pretty figure.

The alternative to the National Policy was freer trade with the United States – or perhaps even completely free trade with the great republic.

That, claimed critics of the Liberal Party, could lead to commercial, and later, political domination of Canada by the United States. Trade policy was regarded as having fundamental political significance. Many Canadians remembered that economic union had preceded the political unification of Germany in 1870.

PUCK.

"IT'S ONLY A QUESTION OF TIME."

OLD FOGYISM MAY HOLD HER BACK FOR A WHILE, BUT SHE IS BOUND TO COME TO US.

Free trade or commercial union with the United States was seen as a threat to Canada's existence as a separate federation. This problem has never been solved, and has been debated by Canadians for over one hundred years.

"It's only a question of time."
Old Fogyism may hold her back for a while, but she is bound to come to us.

149

THE WAY HE W...
CANADA...

PUBLISHED BY THE INDUSTRIAL L...

JLD LIKE IT.

OR SALE.

REDERIC NICHOLLS, HON. SEC.

TORONTO LITH Co

Conservatives and their business allies played up free trade as a threat to Canadian independence. They argued that the Liberal Party wanted to sell Canada to the United States.

In this poster, Sir Richard Cartwright is about to surrender an enslaved and innocent Canada to a gleeful Uncle Sam. The price was a bag of gold, which would no doubt be used to elect a Liberal government which would, of course, serve American interests.

As the pressures mounted, the Government became weaker.

Macdonald was now an old man, but refused to retire. He was seventy-six when he called the crucial election of 1891.

Opposing him was Wilfrid Laurier, Liberal Party leader since 1887.

Laurier, a youthful fifty, concentrated on economic policy and supported reciprocity with the United States.

It was a dirty election.

The Liberals, led by
Laurier and Cartwright,
campaigned for free
trade with the United
States. In their view, the
Conservatives' National
Policy had failed.

The Conservatives
pulled out all the stops.
Free trade meant
economic integration with
a far stronger partner,
they said. Canada would
lose control of her
economy, and we would
become American
puppets.

Their implication was
clear. The policy of the
Liberal Party was
actually a programme for
treason. Laurier and
Cartwright were
portrayed not only as
traitors, but as bunglers
and fools, outman-
oeuvred by Sir John at
every turn.

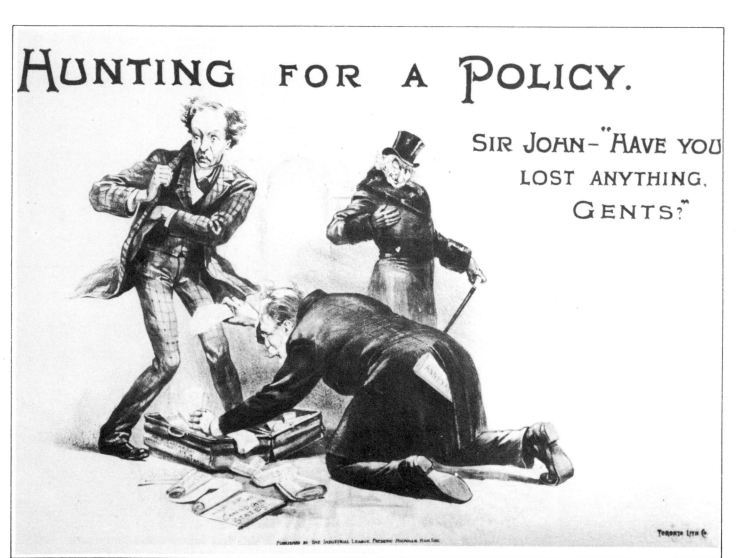

Sir John A. was presented in glowing terms as the Canadians' best friend. From farm to factory, he had their interests at heart.

His National Policy would give Canada both independence and prosperity. The Conservative slogan in 1891 was the finest in Canadian history: "The Old Flag, The Old Policy, The Old Leader."

Convinced that Canada's soul was at stake, Macdonald waged the fight of his life.

He turned the campaign into a straight test of patriotism.

"As for myself," he declared, "my course is clear. A British subject I was born, and a British subject I will die. With my utmost effort, with my latest breath, will I oppose the 'veiled treason' which attempts by sordid means and mercenary proffers to lure our people from their allegiance."

Mowat broke Liberal unity.

So effective was his platform that even Oliver Mowat, his former law student and Ontario's perennial Liberal Premier, was forced to side with Canada against policies that might destroy it.

Mowat's actions demonstrated that Liberalism was not united behind Laurier and Cartwright.

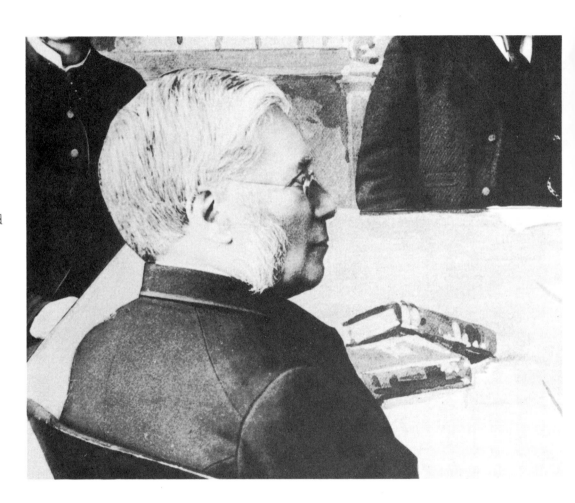

Cartoonists took full advantage of Mowat's reluctance to support economic continentalism.

"Canada is like an apple
    on a tree just beyond reach…
    let it alone, and in due time
    it will fall into our hands."

–James G. Blaine, U.S. Secretary of State

Macdonald was convinced that the Liberals were shaking the tree and the Americans were waiting below to catch the ripe fruit. Canada, he felt, must be saved from the Liberals and their American allies.

He struggled on with his campaign.

Macdonald addressing a night gathering during his last campaign

But in February he collapsed.

The election would be difficult, and the pace was difficult. At Napanee, Ontario, he gave out. But after all the campaigning was over, he triumphed once again.

Sir John had won four elections in a row. Is it any wonder he was called **Fox Populi**, a playful use of the term, **vox populi**: voice of the people.

Rallying after his collapse, Macdonald overcame his exhaustion.

On election day, March 5, 1891, he enjoyed his final political triumph. He attended the new session of the House of Commons with his son, Hugh John, who was now the Member of Parliament for Winnipeg.

Sir John A. Macdonald died on June 6, 1891.

What is the legacy of this great man? His achievements are impressive:

☐ He created the Conservative Party to unite the country, and succeeded.

☐ His government was responsible for the National Policy.

☐ He built the CPR, the transcontinental railroad.

☐ Under his leadership, Canada expanded from the Atlantic to the Pacific, and north to the Arctic.

But his greatest achievement was Canada itself. Sir John A. Macdonald was the founder of his country.

Previous page: Sir John's empty and draped desk in the House of Commons

If his public achievements were great, much of his private life had been sadness, misery, and despair.
☐ For most of his life, he was a victim of the bottle.
☐ His first wife died after a long and painful illness.
☐ His first son, John Alexander, Jr., died in infancy.
☐ He was unable to be a proper father to his surviving son, Hugh John.
☐ Although his son did become Premier of Manitoba, he was hardly a success in public life.
☐ His grandson, John Alexander III, died before reaching manhood.

After his death, Lady Macdonald, created Baroness Macdonald of Earnscliffe by Queen Victoria, chose not to stay in Canada. She took the handicapped Mary to England where they lived out their lives.

Even their furniture and
other household goods
were sold at public
auction the following
spring.

EARNSCLIFFE SALE

COMPLETE LIST OF

**Furniture, china, and glassware, pictures,
ornaments, etc,**

The property of the

Late Right Hon. Sir John A. Macdonald

to be sold at EARNSCLIFFE,   OTTAWA.

Commencing Tuesday 15th May next at 10 a. m.

W H. LEWIS, Auctioneer.

Without "Old Tomorrow" the Conservative Party did not fare well. After 1891, it went through a serious leadership crisis.

Four men gave brief service as Prime Minister: J.J.C. Abbott served in 1891-92, followed by John Thompson, who died in 1894. Then came the hapless Sir Mackenzie Bowell.

Finally, in 1896, the party turned to Charles Tupper, but it was too late. The Conservative reign was over.

Left to right: Abbott and Bowell

Wilfrid Laurier won a
dramatic victory for the
Liberals in 1896.
He was Macdonald's real
political successor. The
new Prime Minister took
the National Policy and
the policies of settlement
and expansion, and
presided over one of
Canada's golden ages.
Laurier remained in
power for fifteen years.

When Sir John died, those who loved him wore a fabric lapel ribbon. He deserved the love of his contemporaries and the respect of generations to follow.

This country is his monument.

In Memoriam

SIR·JOHN MACDONALD, G.C.B.

DIED JUNE, 6TH 1891.

If I had influence over the minds of the people of Canada, any power over their intellect, I would leave them with this legacy:

Whatever you do adhere to the Union–
we are a great country,
and shall become one of the greatest in the universe
if we preserve it;
we shall sink into insignificance and adversity
if we suffer it to be broken.
God and nature have made the two Canadas one–
let no factious men be allowed to put them asunder.

–Sir John A. Macdonald

Index

Abbott, John Joseph Caldwell, 103, 104, 169
Allan, Sir Hugh, 102–104, 108, 115
Bellevue House, 28–33
Blake, Edward, 116, 145, 146
Bowell, Sir Mackenzie, 169
Brown, George, 46, 89, 101
Cameron, John Hillyard, 42, 108
Campbell, Alexander, 44, 114
Canadian Pacific Railway, 102, 115, 118, 127–133, 141
Carling, John, 42
Cartier, George Etienne, 43, 46, 112, 113
Cartwright, Richard, 117, 147, 151, 154
Cataraqui Cemetery, 16
Charlottetown Conference, 47
Civil War (American), 51–55
Clark, Isabella, 27
Dufferin, Lord, 110, 111
Earnscliffe, 82, 83, 87, 168
Elgin, Lord, 45
Fenians, 53, 57
Fort Garry, 92, 97
funeral, 14–20, 22, 165, 172, 173
Great Seal of Canada, 61
Howe, Joseph, 90
Hudson's Bay Company, 91, 96
Laurier, Wilfrid, 22, 120, 121, 144, 153, 154, 170, 171
law career, 25, 26, 119
Lincoln, Abraham, 51
London Conference, 50, 59
loo, 26
Macdonald, Hugh John, 34, 163
Macdonald, John Sandfield, 88, 89
Macdonald, Lady Agnes, 79–81, 101, 137

Macdonald, Mary, 85–87
McDougall, William, 93, 96
McGee, Thomas D'Arcy, 57, 58
Mackenzie, Alexander, 115, 116, 118
Mercier, Honoré, 146
Mowat, Oliver, 44, 158, 159
National Policy, 123, 125, 126, 147–151, 155, 156
Pacific Scandal, 102, 109, 112, 117, 122
Parliament Buildings, construction, 70–77, 115
Quebec Conference, 49, 50
residence: Kingston, 20, 23, 24
         Ottawa, 82
         Toronto, 119
Responsible Government, 45
Riel, Louis/Riel Rebellion, 94–96, 98–100, 139–145
Rose, John, 37
Scott, Thomas, 98
Thompson, John Sparrow David, 138, 169
Tilley, Leonard, 48
Tupper, Charles, 48, 90, 138, 169

Photo Credits

All photographs courtesy of the Public Archives of Canada, Ottawa, except for the following: Queen's University Archives, 13, 18–24, 28, 38–40, 47, 49, 59, 60, 82, 101, 117, 133, 168, 173. Canadian Pacific Corporate Archives, 130–131. Public Archives of Ontario, 44. Manitoba Archives, 97, 98. Hudson's Bay Company, 91, 92. The Ontario Publishing Company Ltd., 161. The Library of Congress, 52, 53, 55. The National Archives, Washington, D.C., 51, 54. Cathy Van Baren, 119. John Brebner, 18, 20, 173, 175. Bellevue House, 29–33.

The type used in this book is Memphis Extra Light with Medium and was set by Typsettra Limited.
The book was prepared for lithography by Champlain Graphics. Printed and bound in Canada by The Bryant Press Limited on 80 lb. Plainfield Offset.